PRESENTATION AS WAR

BY CHUCK BOYER & BILL DUNNE

"The secret of war lies in the communications."

– NAPOLEON BONAPARTE

Book design, illustrations and layout by
Spotlight Creative, LLC*.

info@spotlightcreative.com | 281.970.3800
11123 McCracken Circle, Cypress, Texas 77429
www.spotlightcreative.com

FOREWORD

YOU DON'T HAVE TO BE ANOTHER GEORGE PATTON, NAPOLEON BONAPARTE, LORD NELSON, OR FIELD MARSHAL MONTGOMERY TO RALLY THE TROOPS. BUT YOU CAN USE THEIR TACTICAL INSTINCTS TO HONE YOUR PRESENTATION SKILLS.

This book is for team leaders, task-force point people, managers, directors and vice presidents—the people who don't usually make State of the Union addresses but who are called upon to make those bread-and-butter presentations that drive an organization forward.

The big secret in business (and perhaps in life generally) is not to be a great communicator, but to make people great believers in what you have to say.

You can do this by approaching every presentation the way you would plan and execute a battle—with the goal of winning your battle by winning your audience.

We learn from the brief, forceful and clear messages that Napoleon posted for his troops that any situation, no matter how complex, can be reduced to certain essentials. This is the level that he used to tap the energy and enthusiasm of his troops. Patton, with his earthy speeches, Montgomery with his demand for logic and detail accomplished the same purpose.

> "Wise people learn when they can; fools learn when they must."
>
> – FIELD MARSHAL ARTHUR WELLESLEY, DUKE OF WELLINGTON

1

Lord Nelson, the British admiral who won the strategic naval battle of Trafalgar in 1805, signaled the simplest of messages to his officers and men before the battle: "England expects every man to do his duty."

Language that plain tends to be out of the ordinary in a business meeting today. But it should not be. There are striking parallels between great military communications and great business presentations. And what we, the authors, have learned from these military leaders, and from our own combined 45 years of writing presentations and papers for business managers and senior executives, is the basis for this book. We have also drawn upon our own experiences with basic small-unit infantry tactics that we are familiar with from our post-college experiences in the Army Rangers and Marine Corps.

This book, in other words, seeks to arm you for your next presentation assignment with fresh thinking based on infantry warfare tactics. And we do stress tactics rather than strategy. These are step-by-step tactics on how to take the field—the stage, the podium, the front of the room—and win the battle to have your thoughts and ideas find a place in the minds, and maybe even the hearts, of your audience.

Why *Presentation as War*? Reverential audiences are rare and getting rarer. Even audiences comprising your own company employees don't necessarily trust you anymore—if they ever did. Business has always had a healthy atmosphere of competitive edginess. But today, no matter how big or small your presentation, your audience is no longer "your" audience. Any presentation can result in a skirmish, or even rise to the level of a full-blown battle. There are many reasons why.

When you speak to an audience today, you represent, at that moment, one point of view in an extended community of many points of view—a live, virtual community that includes your customers and suppliers and partners, as well as competitors and industry experts. As you are speaking, the audience has access to hundreds and thousands of points of view: information and opinions from all over the world.

Every audience, from a staff meeting of a dozen people to a customer-supplier extravaganza of 3,000, is a global audience. Your job is to capture that moment, seize the attention of those market-state players, and win them to your side, to your opinion—to your goals. More than ever before, you will have to defeat an array of natural enemies: opposing points of view, perceptions, prejudice, doubt, distractions, distrust, and sheer boredom. And these "enemies" are more formidable than at any time in the history of business.

By combining basic principles of presentation with the basic principles of small-unit infantry tactics, we put you on a time scale measured in minutes and seconds. Just as in a real battle, every move you make has a consequence, often an immediate one. Everything you do, large or small, counts. This book is about tactics. The advice is hands-on, real time; do this, do not do that.

Fealty and respect flow to those who demonstrate the value and relevance of their thinking, their accomplishments, and their leadership. Every presentation is a battle to gain ground on these terms.

This book provides a new perspective and a new set of tools to help you win those battles.

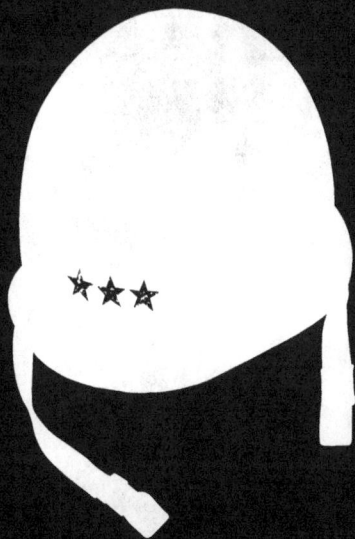

TABLE OF CONTENTS

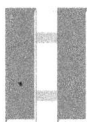

CHAPTER ONE:
IT NEVER WAS EASY.
NOW IT'S A BATTLE.

"I gave one who was cowering a smart rap over the backside with the flat of my sword—and stood with my revolver and swore I'd shoot the first who ran or fired against orders."

— OLIVER WENDELL HOLMES, JR.,
Future Supreme Court Justice writing to his parents as a young infantry lieutenant after the Battle of Fair Oaks, near Richmond, Virginia, June 1862

CHAPTER ONE:
IT NEVER WAS EASY.
NOW IT'S A BATTLE.

INDEED, IT NEVER WAS EASY.

But when you stand to speak today you face two enemies: a business climate of anxiety and distrust, and the audience's ability with their smart phones to communicate among themselves in real time— perhaps cutting your remarks to ribbons, quietly, unobtrusively— even as you speak.

Your audience will almost always be a mixture of types: people for you, people against you, people who understand what you're talking about, people who don't, people who don't care one way or the other, and some who would rather be someplace else. As prominent Wall Street speechwriter Joan Chevalier puts it: "Business audiences today are looking to get you one way or another. They use good information to move beyond you, and bad information to mothball you."

When Lou Gerstner took over IBM in 1993, the fabled company had suffered near mortal wounds—many by its own hand. It was bleeding billions of dollars and 82 years of glory and goodwill. Worse, from an employee point of view, Gerstner was the first outsider to take over the top job at IBM. And the first presentation in which he was involved was perhaps the most influential of his IBM career. It was made not by him but by one of his senior vice presidents.

As Gerstner recalls the event in his book, *Who Says Elephants Can't Dance?*: "One of the first meetings I asked for was a briefing on the state of [our mainframe] business. At that time, the standard format of any important IBM meeting was a presentation using overhead projectors and graphics on transparencies that IBMers called—and no one remembers why—'foils' [the equivalent of today's ubiquitous PowerPoint slides]."

As he tells it, "[The head of IBM's mainframe business] was on his second foil when I stepped to the table and, as politely as I could in front of his team, switched off the projector. After a long moment of awkward silence, I simply said, 'Let's just talk about your business.'"

Literally within minutes, emails about Gerstner's turning off the "slides" had circled the globe to IBM's 400,000 employees. "It was as if," he said, "the President of the United States had banned the use of English at White House meetings."

What Gerstner did in that moment was take control of the battlefield. It wasn't a victory. It was an opening shot that told his audience that he was taking control. He still had a lot of work to do, in fact several years worth of work. But he had his audience sitting up straight, paying attention, and subconsciously weighing the risk of putting up a fight. He was on his way.

So there you stand, in front of a group of people who are neutral at best and hostile at worst. In addition—with email, IM, text messaging, Twitter, and a growing assortment of social media "gathering points"— they are armed to the teeth. They can whip themselves into riot mode. Your suit will be described as "empty," your presentation as "content free." And these are just the things we can print.

WHAT CAN YOU DO?

If making a presentation is seen as combat, and if the goal of your presentation is to capture or gain control of the battlefield, then you can use small-unit combat tactics to achieve your goal.

On a real battlefield, the desired sequence runs like this:

1 Reconnoiter to assess enemy strength, positions, and capabilities.

2 Develop a plan of attack by choosing either a surprise attack or battlefield preparation.

3 Rehearse your attack plan.

4 Execute the attack with speed and force.

5 Commit your reserve forces if necessary.

6 Secure your objective, and prepare for a possible counterattack.

7 Declare victory and rally the troops for the next mission.

This book shows how these basic battlefield techniques can work for you when making a speech or presentation. Using these guidelines, we demonstrate how to "capture" your audience and "win" them to your side. We show you how to subdue and neutralize audience members who are reluctant to be won over.

Whether or not you're considered a gifted speaker, you can be seen as well-armed and even a tad dangerous. Without knowing why, your audience will pay attention because they will be on your side; and if not on your side they will sense that the risk of not paying attention to you could be harmful to them. And once you have their attention and respect, your battle is more than half won.

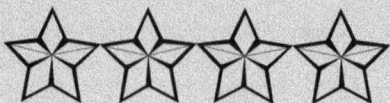

GENERAL WILLIAM TECUMSEH SHERMAN

We lay before you the case of General William Tecumseh Sherman, one of the best and toughest (and in some places the most notorious) generals of the American Civil War.

A good, if a bit unruly, student at West Point (three years ahead of his future commanding officer, Ulysses S. Grant) Sherman never saw the flame and smoke of battle until he found himself in the middle of the largest battle in the opening months of the Civil War, the First Battle of Bull Run. The Confederates carried the day at Bull Run, and the Yankees left the field in panic. Sherman was one of the few green Yankee generals who stood his ground, but the experience shook him to the core. A few months later, in fact, he had what today we'd call a nervous breakdown. He had to leave the Army for a few weeks to regain his wits.

But he did return, though more eager to serve under his junior friend Grant than to take full responsibility on his own shoulders. He distinguished himself on the first day of the two-day bloody Battle of Shiloh, holding the field with his division against more numerous Confederate units. Wounded twice, he never left the field. He helped Grant turn the tide from defeat to victory on the second day. He went on to help Grant win the important Battle of Vicksburg, and eventually became the commanding general for all U.S. troops in the Western theater of the war. His brilliant campaign to capture the key city of Atlanta, Georgia, saved lives on both sides, using maneuver and strategy more than blunt, head-on combat.

"All men naturally shrink from pain and danger, and only incur their risk from some higher motive, or from habit; so that I would define true courage to be a perfect sensibility of the measure of danger, and a mental willingness to incur it, rather than that insensibility to danger of which I have heard far more than I have seen. The most courageous men are generally unconscious of possessing the quality; therefore, when one professes it too openly, by words or bearing, there is reason to mistrust it.

I would further illustrate my meaning by describing a man of true courage to be one who possesses all his faculties and senses perfectly when serious danger is actually present."

— GENERAL WILLIAM TECUMSEH SHERMAN

By the end of the war, he was clearly viewed as the second most important Yankee General. Some say he accomplished more than Grant did. His troops grew to love and respect him, calling him "Uncle Billy."

Sherman himself wrote a lengthy analysis of war after his long four years on the battlefield of the Civil War.

And from his lessons learned we draw the following inspirations for presenters:

1 You can do things that at first seem wildly overwhelming to you.

2 By the discipline of habit, preparation, rehearsal, and the actual experience of improving your presentations, you can become good at it—even under the most difficult conditions.

3 When you fail, and fail badly, fully believe, even in the depths of your discouragement, that you will recover, you will come back, and you will succeed.

CHAPTER TWO:
RECONNOITER.

"Battles are won by slaughter and maneuver. The greater the general, the more he contributes in maneuver, the less he demands in slaughter."

- WINSTON CHURCHILL

CHAPTER TWO:
RECONNOITER:
KNOW YOUR AUDIENCE AS YOU WOULD KNOW YOUR ENEMY.

CONDUCT A THOROUGH RECONNAISSANCE TO ASSESS ENEMY STRENGTH, POSITIONS, AND CAPABILITIES.

> *"After we had secured the opening of a line over which to bring our supplies to the army, I made a personal inspection to see the situation of the pickets of the two armies... As I would be under short-range fire and in an open country, I took nobody with me, except a bugler, who stayed some distance to the rear."*

– MEMOIRS OF GEN. ULYSSES S. GRANT,

on his reconnaissance just prior to the Battle of Chattanooga, 1863

If leaders such as Grant and Sherman can take the risk and the trouble to personally inspect a potential battlefield, why not you?

What does the likely battleground look like? Is it flat or hilly? Dry or swampy? Open or forested? What time of day is the encounter likely to occur? What phase will the moon be in? Who will have the sun in their eyes? Are there streams, valleys, ravines? Any one of these factors can determine the tactics needed to win.

In speeches and presentations, the battleground consists of the thinking and attitudes of your audience, and reconnaissance is essential. If it's an internal company presentation, you will probably know the ground quite well. Sometimes too well. The same old faces, maybe a few contractors, occasionally some self-important hot shot from headquarters. Even presentations to outside groups—to customers, to professional and trade groups—will often be made in front of many familiar faces.

> **"I have many a time crept forward to the skirmish-line to avail myself of the cover of the pickets' "little fort," to observe more closely some expected result."**
>
> **- MEMOIRS OF GEN. WM. TECUMSEH SHERMAN,**
> *American Civil War*

Though you may know the people well, their thoughts and feelings change constantly. You need to get out and do a thorough reconnaissance on what's going on in their heads. You need to get out there and separate the Problems and Solutions, on the one hand, from the Issues and Expectations, on the other. Say that again?

Let's start with an example. Your team has just fouled up the quality on an important product. A division VP has "asked" you to put together a presentation explaining how your team will correct the problem and what it will do to prevent it from happening again. The audience will comprise representatives from the four departments you work with every day, plus a couple of corporate "types" from Quality Control, and some new guy sitting in from your boss's boss's team.

You're thinking: "We found the problem. We were using an old spec, and everyone else was working with a new spec. We've updated our specs, and we put in place a regular, repeatable process to ensure that this doesn't happen again. We found the problem, we solved it. We have a solution, the solution works, case closed."

Not quite. You decide to ride out to the front lines to do a thorough reconnaissance. Why? Because the battlefield is a fluid place; its features and contours can change in a flash. You just might turn up a startling piece of new news. While you and your team are busy working Problem and Solution, the audience you are preparing to address has started thinking Issue and Expectation.

What is Issue and Expectation? It is simply a larger, broader view of the Problem and Solution. It's often that internal voice we hear asking ourselves, "What's really going on here?" In most cases, when you dig into the minds of your audiences, you will discover that they are not thinking about things in terms of a specific problem and its solution. They already take it as a given that you are going to find the problem and fix it.

The issue that's really on their minds is that your team has a reputation for dropping the ball, and the expectation in their minds is that they will continue to drop the ball periodically, even after they have fixed this one instance of the problem. This is what's going on inside the minds of the departments that depend on you, as well as some of your own people.

THAT'S WHERE THE REAL BATTLE LINES ARE FORMING.

To win this battle you have to make that reconnaissance and learn what the audience is thinking. Once you've successfully done that, your approach to this battle will change. Getting up and presenting the problem—which everyone already knows about—and then showing the standard solutions—which everyone also already knows about—won't cut it.

You've got to address the problem and solution, of course. But you've got to do it in a way that wins the Issue-and-Expectation battle.

This is not limited to events where something has gone wrong. New product announcements, marketing and advertising rollouts, organizational changes, policy changes, and especially strategy changes—all are affected by the narrow Problem-Solution effect and the larger Issue-Expectation view of the world.

LET'S LOOK AT ANOTHER EXAMPLE FROM THE REAL WORLD.

You have a new advertising and marketing campaign to roll out. There will be advertising at the national level, supplemented by marketing materials generated for each customer segment. Your company does at least one of these every year, sometimes two or three. In the run-up to these campaigns there are *always* a lot of changes, and *generally* a lot of last-minute budget cuts and pull-backs. What looked great at the concept stage begins to feel tentative as you get ready to roll it out. The hard details of real life tend to muck things up. Current sales and quality issues, competitive changes, customer flux—all these things get in the way of the once seamless plans made for the next big project.

Over time, your troops and all the agencies and support groups you work with have gotten used to this pattern of big expectations followed by days and nights of a thousand paper cuts, leading to a modified, much more modest rollout. So everyone, including perhaps yourself, has fallen into a pattern of "expecting lower expectations." This is the mind-set you have to get out and reconnoiter.

Hence, these are typical "Issue" situations you have to look for on your reconnaissance missions:

1. Are the people to whom you will be presenting already discounting what they are going to hear from you?

2. Does your presentation look like it's falling into a predictable cycle?

3. Does the audience think you may not be the one calling the real

RECONNAISSANCE TIPS

1 Talk to at least a couple of prospective audience members. Find out what concerns them most in their businesses. What worries them?

2 Talk to the sponsoring party.

3 Get your hands on the full program or agenda. Note the time slot you're in. Before lunch or after lunch? Before a coffee break or after?

4 Find out who the speakers were at previous events of this nature, and what the tone was. Annually recurring events usually develop a distinctive "tone" that audiences expect to see repeated.

5 Identify the speakers on the program before you and after you.

6 Note the day of the week: Is it a Monday, when many in the audience will be thinking about what's waiting for them back at the office? Or a Thursday or Friday, when minds are starting to let go of work-week worries.

shots, so that what you have to tell them doesn't carry that much weight?

4 Does your audience suspect that nothing you can tell them will even modestly change the course of their daily work?

5 Does the audience know who you are, either in title or in context?

6 Determine how important it might be for you to demonstrate your authority, either as a manager or a technical expert, before delving into the heart of your presentation. This is a common problem in many "mid-level" technical presentations. Some in the audience, namely those who don't know you well, will wonder whether or not you really know your stuff.

As successful advertising people have long known, you must structure your presentation from your audience's point of view. If you don't start with where they are, you can't lead them somewhere else.

This brings up an important step in your reconnaissance: you need to find out what information people have received from other sources in the last few days or weeks. That means staying in tune with what's going on in the relevant parts of your own company, as well as in the marketplace—including competitors.

One more caveat: You should not be satisfied with just a general image of your audience. You need to focus on the 20 percent who do 80 percent of the work or who command 80 percent of the attention or who generate 80 percent of the opinions.

At times you may need only be concerned with the thinking of just two or three key "tipping-point" people who will be in your audience. Knowing what they think will allow you to structure your presentation to begin with their point of view—even if you intend to blow them out of the water with your point of view.

This is exactly what military officers think about during reconnaissance. Who am I up against? What do I know about this guy? How has he reacted in the past? What is he up to today? If I do this, what will he think I'm doing, and how will he react?

PHYSICAL RECONNAISSANCE

No professional military officer, like no professional entertainer, would think of mounting a battle or a stage without a physical reconnaissance. Stumbling around in front of an audience because conditions aren't what you expected invites an immediate decline in attention, credibility, and respect. Just seeing the type of podium or speaker platform you'll be using will go a long way toward your mental preparation for speaking. This holds as true for old hands as it does for greenhorns.

Go to the place where you will be presenting. Stand where you will stand. Move around the way you expect to move during the presentation, and check the technical details.

PICKING YOUR TARGET, KNOWING YOUR PURPOSE

Countless speeches and presentations are wasted because the speaker sets his sights on the wrong *target*. This results most often from confusing the target with the *topic*. Your *topic* can be about almost anything, but as to your *targets*, there are basically only three:

1 Emotions

2 Beliefs

3 Behaviors

Because humans are only human, every audience will be an embodiment of all three. But only one should predominate in your thoughts as you formulate your presentation tactics. Should you appeal mostly to their emotions, their beliefs, or their behaviors? What's it going to be?

It could be all three. Go to Shakespeare's *Julius Caesar* and flip through to Marc Antony's speech to his "friends, Romans, countrymen" as he mourns over Caesar's corpse. Marc Antony is the rabble rouser extraordinaire as he plucks at the audience's emotions, beliefs, and behaviors. Ultimately, though, we realize that his main target is the audience's behavior. His purpose is to change that behavior from one of docile acceptance of the bloody assassination to one of wrathful frenzy, and to set them off with torches and pitchforks against Brutus and the gang. Similarly, anyone making a presentation today must think ahead and keep firmly in mind what his ultimate purpose is.

Purpose, very handily, comes in one of three flavors. Your purpose can be either to:

1 Confirm

2 Challenge

3 Change

Thus the complete analysis of picking your target and deciding on your purpose comes down to a few simple questions:

■ Is your purpose to confirm the audience in their emotions? To challenge their emotions? Or to change their emotions?

■ Is your purpose to confirm their beliefs? To challenge their beliefs? Or to change their beliefs?

■ Is your purpose to confirm their behaviors? To challenge their behaviors? Or to change their behaviors?

But your purpose, like your target, may also be a mixture, especially if your audience is made up of varied constituencies: customers alongside business partners alongside suppliers, for example. But as with your target selection, one purpose should predominate. One of the chief tasks of reconnaissance is to decide what that should be. This exercise of picking your target and crystallizing your purpose can be enormously helpful to your success. It is useful not only in determining the content of your presentation—what goes in and what stays out— but also in avoiding a huge mistake that could doom the whole effort.

Take the real-life example of a senior executive of a major national bank who accepted an invitation to speak to a gathering of public school administrators. Nice opportunity, he thought, *I'll get to tell them about the business practices that make banking operations run so smoothly. I'll tell them how those business practices might be adapted to improve the performance of public schools.* He had targeted their beliefs about school operations. His purpose was to challenge or change those beliefs.

After much preparation, the day of the event arrives, and our hero discovers that the audience is not just school administrators. It's also local business and civic leaders. Moreover, the point of the gathering—the purpose—was to celebrate many years of business and public-school cooperation. It was essentially a rah-rah meeting, organized on expectations of celebration and good feelings. Which is to say, emotions.

Too late to alter his presentation, our bank executive plods through his prepared remarks and sits down to a smattering of polite applause. Big flop. The result of poor targeting, misunderstood purpose, bad reconnaissance.

FINAL WORD

If you are an experienced executive, you have probably made presentations that you created with only a cursory view as to what your audience might be thinking. You've sat through hundreds of such presentations yourself.

Presentations are "live" events. In a way they are contests, not unlike a skirmish on a battlefield. And just as it happens on the battlefield, the enemy and your audience have a say in the outcome. Reconnaissance, while never perfect, is the first step in winning the battle.

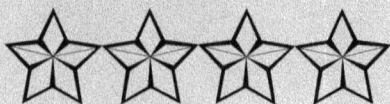

GENERAL ULYSSES S. GRANT

Cadet Grant was an indifferent student at West Point in the 1840s. By his own account, he preferred to read novels and ride horses. The dry study of infantry and artillery tactics failed to hold his attention. Going to West Point in the first place had been his father's idea, not his.

But less than 20 years later, at the outset of the American Civil War, he found himself leading a regiment of infantry—more than a thousand men in total—on a march to engage Confederate soldiers. Lying in his pup tent at night studying the infantry manual, he desperately tried to absorb the lessons he had skipped over earlier in his career. He decided that the exercise was futile, and determined that he would make up his tactics and plans as he went along.

The opportunity to improvise on the fly came just a few days later. As his regiment approached a small hill, word came back that the Confederate unit was in a small valley just on the other side of the hill. Grant tried to remember the specific command to change the line of order from a narrow marching formation to a wider line of battle. But he couldn't. Nor could he muster the presence of mind to bring his marching soldiers to a halt before they crested the hill and exposed themselves to the Confederate soldiers on the other side.

The regiment, with Grant leading, marched up the hill and down the other side, untried and unprepared for battle. Fortunately for them, as they crested the hill and headed down into the valley below they saw that the Confederates just hours before had abandoned their campfires and defensive positions and fled.

Grant learned two valuable lessons that day—lessons that would propel him from an unknown Lt. Colonel of Volunteers to the Commanding General of the entire U.S. Army in a matter of two years.

First, he would always have a coordinated plan and a concrete objective for everything he did. Every detail, from bread for his men to forage for the horses and mules would be included. Marches, maneuvers, and attacks would be carried out with all units coordinating and supporting each other. And each unit commander would have a simple, clear objective of what was expected. His emphasis was always on the simple and clear: "If the enemy line in front of you softens, be prepared to advance."

The second major lesson he internalized was that the enemy invariably was as confused and afraid as he was. There was a widely accepted belief in the early months of the Civil War that the southern soldiers and generals were vastly superior to anything the North could muster—a belief supported by the North's poor showing on the battlefield. The Northern Army of the Potomac in the Eastern part of the United States did not win a major battle until mid-1863, two and a half years into the war.

Grant knew, from thoroughly studying his enemy (he had gone to West Point with many of the Confederate generals, and had served with them earlier, in the Mexican War) that the enemy possessed no unusual or superior powers. They were soldiers just like his own, some good, some not so good. From that point on, he spent nearly all his time and energy concentrating on his objectives, and far less time worrying about what the enemy might or might not do to him.

He knew them by name, by reputation, and by examples of what they had accomplished or failed to accomplish when they had all served together in an earlier war, against Mexico. He knew their strengths and weaknesses.

If, through your reconnaissance, you learn nearly as much about your audience as Grant knew about his enemy, then you will be able to concentrate on your objective, comfortable that what you have to say will be well received by the men and women who will invest their time listening to you.

CHAPTER THREE:

DEVELOP A PLAN OF ATTACK.

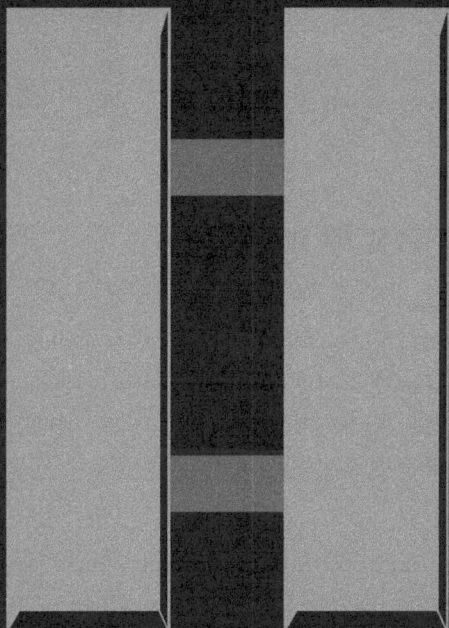

"Given the same amount of intelligence, timidity will do a thousand times more damage than audacity."

— CARL VON CLAUSEWITZ,
Prussian military general and theorist

CHAPTER THREE:
DEVELOP A
PLAN OF ATTACK.

YOU HAVE TWO ALTERNATIVES: SOFTEN UP THE BATTLEFIELD—OR A SURPRISE ATTACK.

Do you prepare a surprise attack?—one that will startle your audience and capture their attention? Or do you begin with long-range battlefield preparations, telling your audience where we've been, where we are, and where we are heading—before unloading your main attack: "How we plan to get there."

Advantages and disadvantages attach to both types of attack. Let's consider them, starting with the essential key message, such as:

> *"This is the end of the second quarter. The first half has been a bust. Hence, we're changing the strategy, and we're changing a number of the key players. And we're going to meet or exceed our targets in the second half—or else."*

Here we hit the audience cold with the changes that will be taking place as we enter the third and fourth quarters. Now that we have their unwavering attention, we back up and tell them why these rather dramatic changes are being made.

The Surprise-Attack Format looks like this:

A   Shocking news

B   Reasoning behind it

C   What happens now and what is expected tomorrow.

With the alternative—which is the Soften-up-the-Battlefield approach—we begin by recalling what we had set out to do at the beginning of the first quarter. We show the results of quarters one and two. And we make it clear that we failed to meet our targets and by how much. Having softened them up, we unload what they already suspect: Changes will be made and we will not fail in the second half.

The Soften-up-the-Battlefield Format looks like this:

A Here's what we had planned to do

B Here's what happened and why

C Here are the changes we're making and here is what is expected tomorrow.

The more difficult part of formulating the plan-of-attack decision comes when you analyze the pros and cons of each approach.

SURPRISE-ATTACK PROS:

1 If the audience is already leaning in your direction or deferential to your point of view, the Surprise Attack can be highly effective in getting your message across. Just be sure that you have a hand to play and that the audience knows you, respects you, and looks to you for guidance.

2 The Surprise Attack can be useful if the audience knows you fairly well and might be jaded because you're a "predictable" commodity. Just the act of committing yourself to the Surprise Attack mode will change the nature and feel of your presentation. Veteran observers in your audience will sense the difference, and their reactions will be picked up by the rest of the audience. (Audiences are intensely susceptible to peer reactions—a lesson learned from ancient Greek theater more than 2000 years ago.) If you "get to" enough people in your audience, the entire audience will be with you. The converse is equally true.

SURPRISE-ATTACK CONS:

1 It can come off as unnecessarily brutal, thus alienating some audience members who might have been neutral or leaning toward you. There's enough drama in their lives right now.

2 Using a Surprise Attack on a neutral or negative-leaning audience requires that you maintain a strong attack all the way through the battle. Any sign of weakness or slowing down after the initial surprise has worn off can give the audience the mental room they need to regroup and turn you off or turn against you.

SOFTEN-UP-THE-BATTLEFIELD PROS:

1 Making a step-by-step case before coming to the key message can be seen by many as a sign of respect for their intelligence and knowledge. If the audience knows you well, they have a good idea of what you are up to and why. Your background development will help them come to the same conclusion that you are going to come to when you get to your key message.

2 If you are a spellbinding speaker with a real gift—the kind of person people love to listen to no matter what the subject— then Soften up the Battlefield can often be the best choice for guiding your audience in the direction you want. That's a very big "if," however.

SOFTEN-UP-THE-BATTLEFIELD CONS:

1 A slowly developing presentation gives the audience time for competing thoughts...such as, "Why am I sitting here listening to all this? What's his point?"

2 Smart, active, charge-ahead audiences may already know all the background material you are showing them. They may wonder why you are telling them something they already know.

Surprise Attack is good for audiences who are tough-minded, aggressive, play-to-win types. They will often like a bold surprise attack, wishing that they had thought of it themselves. Who are these audiences?:

A Sales people

B Financial analysts/ Industry analysts

C Business leaders

> **"The Surprise Attack is good for audiences who are tough-minded, aggressive, play-to-win types."**

Softening up the Battlefield is good for audiences who are sensitive, highly intelligent, or slightly wounded. Who are these audiences?:

A R&D, Staff and Manufacturing people, and academics of all kinds

B Very large mixed audiences

C Any group that knows the world is not going their way

Some speakers are simply more suited for one approach than the other, and there is simply no "real" choice in the matter.

Let's look at examples from history. When Margaret Thatcher was elected to leadership of the British Conservative Party in 1975 and later became the first woman Prime Minister, she wasted no time in laying out her plan to push Great Britain away from socialism and back to productive capitalism.

Less than a minute into her first landmark speech she said, quite directly, "Our problem is not that we have too little Socialism. It is that we have too much." From there she went on to develop the arguments for her case. Her Surprise-Attack method was well received.

Famous American businessman and presidential advisor Bernard Baruch was appointed as the first U.S. representative to the United Nations Atomic Energy Commission in 1946. In his presentation to the Commission on how to control atomic weapons he began: "We are here to make a choice between the quick and the dead. That is our business." He used Surprise Attack in his speech to try to prevent surprise attacks. The speech worked well.

Winston Churchill officially proclaimed the beginning of the Cold War between the Western World and the Soviet Union in his famous "Iron Curtain" speech of 1946 at Fulton College, Missouri. But the Russians had just fought as allies with the Americans and the British to win the War in Europe in 1945. Churchill, therefore, spent some time discussing all that the Russians had done to help win World War II before getting to his key point: things had changed, and an Iron Curtain had descended between the West and the Russian sphere of central European countries. Soften-up-the-Battlefield at its best.

GENERAL OMAR BRADLEY

You don't have to be an accomplished actor to become a respected presenter. George Patton wasn't the only great American "speech maker" of WWII. The quietest and most humble of field generals of that era, Omar Bradley, showed that you need not be a bombastic big mouth to get things done. Bradley almost always said "please," before giving orders. Yet he had nearly one million officers and soldiers under his command—the largest field unit ever commanded by an American general.

A 48-year-old bespectacled former math teacher from West Point, Bradley at the height of World War II looked more like someone's idea of a young grandfather than he did a warrior and a general. But underneath his unassuming temperament, Bradley had the heart and the brain of a great warrior. He commanded the American First Army at Normandy, and the 12th Army Group, comprising four large Armies by the end of the war. He eventually became a five-star general, one of only nine in the history of the U.S. Army, Navy, and Air Force. Along the way he earned the admiration, respect, and even adulation of the men and women who served under him.

In him one could find attributes useful to any leader: he planned meticulously, yet he calculated risks; he treated his senior people with utmost respect, yet he could move quickly and decisively to relieve them of command when he determined they couldn't get the job done; he delegated work effectively, as all managers must, but he also exposed himself to enemy fire to do first-hand reconnaissance and to follow the ebb and flow of battle.

Because he never sought the limelight and never heralded his own accomplishments, Bradley today doesn't have the name or reputation of such glittering, self-illuminated stars as George Patton and Douglas MacArthur. No one has yet thought to make a movie of Bradley's life. But Patton and the other generals understood the effectiveness of Bradley's quiet assertiveness. Patton graduated eight years ahead of Bradley at West Point, and in the early stages of World War II, Bradley reported to Patton. Like the race between the turtle and the hare, though, Bradley eventually passed Patton, and for the last two years of the war, Patton reported to Bradley.

Perhaps nothing illustrates the power of Bradley's manner better than the following story. The co-author of this book, Chuck Boyer, worked at IBM for several years under Colonel Chet Hansen, a senior communications executive at IBM who had served as Bradley's aide-de-camp in World War II. Hansen had been a young reserve Army lieutenant out of Syracuse University when then-Colonel Bradley chose him as an aide. Hansen worked closely with Bradley through the entire four-and-a-half years of the war. Hansen told Boyer the following:

"During the campaign across Sicily, before the American and British Forces invaded the mainland of Italy, I accompanied Gen. Bradley on a reconnaissance trip in his jeep. We were driving toward the front lines, where our troops were fighting the Germans. In the chaos of battle, when a lot of the road signs had been either damaged or destroyed, we lost our way and drove into a small village to get directions. The village had a small square in the center, like many villages, and as we drove up a narrow side street to the square, a small unit of American soldiers signaled us to stop our jeep, get out and take cover. Evidently they were searching for an enemy sniper. The soldiers were crouched all around the square with their eyes on the second and third floor windows of the surrounding buildings. Always willing to pitch in with his men, the General got out and turned to me and said, 'Hand me my carbine.' We kept a small carbine rifle in the back of the jeep. It had been quite a while since I'd had any training with it. As I grabbed it and handed it to the General, I must have knocked the safety from off to on, and hit the trigger at the same time. The rifle went off and the bullet went right past the General's head. The troops in the square, thinking they might have just heard the sniper, immediately opened fire on all the windows of all the buildings in the square. It took a while for all the shooting, the sound of breaking glass and the yelling to quiet down. When calm was finally restored, General Bradley turned to me and said, 'Would you please be more careful.'"

Such was Bradley's impact and reputation that war correspondent Ernie Pyle called him "the soldier's general."

CHAPTER FOUR:
REHEARSE THE ATTACK.

"After we have thought out everything carefully in advance and have sought and found without prejudice the most plausible plan, we must not be ready to abandon it at the slightest provocation."

– CARL VON CLAUSEWITZ

CHAPTER FOUR:
REHEARSE THE ATTACK.

THIS IS WHERE THE BATTLE IS WON—OR LOST.

Clausewitz, the famous Prussian general and military theorist, is right: If you've thought through everything carefully, don't abandon your plan or become alarmed when something goes wrong. If you haven't rehearsed your presentation carefully and often, you haven't thought it through enough, and that leaves you susceptible to booby traps.

We know very well that you will attempt to make presentations with little or almost no rehearsal. This is true particularly if you've been "at the game" for awhile, or if you are giving the third or thirteenth version of essentially the same presentation. What may add to the temptation is the availability of modern speech aids such as teleprompters.

Don't succumb. Plan on nose-to-the-grindstone rehearsals for every presentation. No exceptions. If seasoned stage performers rehearse long and hard before a performance, there must be a good reason. Several good reasons actually.

First off, no one is immune to some measure of stage fright. The most seasoned and confident of speakers can have a sudden attack of nerves, sometimes for no apparent reason, but usually because of a last-minute surprise. It could be that you were expecting to speak to a hundred people, and it turns out to be a thousand. Or you discover that your bitterest rival is on the agenda right after you. It could be something as simple as poor lighting. Or maybe the podium is lacking that lip on the lower edge that keeps your notes from sliding off and dropping to the floor. Whatever it is, your heart rate soars, your legs go wobbly, and your larynx seizes up. No performer—and remember, that's what you are—should be unprepared for some sense of fear when confronting a sea of faces.

> YOU SHOULD REHEARSE TO THE POINT WHERE, IF YOU HAD TO, YOU COULD STAND UP AND GIVE THE IMPORTANT POINTS OF YOUR TALK WITHOUT NOTES, SLIDES, OR CHARTS—JUST YOU ALONE WITH YOUR WELL-REHEARSED MIND.

Rigorous, serious, intensive rehearsal is your armor against such attacks. You should aim to become so familiar with the first few lines or paragraphs of your speech that you can deliver them under duress. That goal by itself is important because getting through the first few sentences unscathed has a calming effect on the nerves.

Rehearsal can also remind you of good arguments made in earlier presentations. It brings out the obvious glitches and rough transitions in a new pitch. It helps you spot the missing transitions that are essential to clarity.

As for any warrior, being in good physical condition is also important, because giving a speech—projecting the energy that will hold an audience's attention for ten, twenty, thirty minutes—actually places high demands on the body.

If you think you are good to go without a rehearsal, compare yourself to Winston Churchill...in his own words:

> *"I spent many hours preparing my discourse and learning it so thoroughly by heart that I could almost have said it backwards in my sleep...being told that I had about a half hour, I confined myself rigorously to twenty-five minutes. I found by repeated*

THE BIGGEST CRUTCH

Wielding a crutch instead of a rifle on the battlefield is not a winning tactic. Neither is relying on slide software (e.g., PowerPoint) as the be-all and end-all of your presentation support.

"There is a way to be quickly taken for the opposite of a leader, and to be typecast within seconds as a dork, a dweeb, a jargon-monkey, a bore," warns Bill Lane, who for 20 years was Jack Welch's speechwriter at GE. "It's called PowerPoint."

experiments with a stop-watch that I could certainly canter over the course in twenty minutes. This would leave time for interruptions. Above all one must not be hurried or flurried. One must not yield too easily to the weakness of audiences. There they were; what could they do? They had asked for it, and they must have it."

And lest we think that Churchill was a great natural orator, we should remember this. He was so frightened during his first several years as a junior member of the British Parliament that he wrote down and memorized several different responses to anticipated questions. Later he would write, after giving a successful but painfully crafted and rehearsed speech in Parliament:

> *"The general verdict was not unfavorable. Although many guessed I had learnt it all by heart, this was pardoned because of the pains I had taken."*

These are the same pains that should be familiar to the speaking life of every serious presenter, such as yourself.

A TRICKY FRIEND

A classic warning on the dangers of relying too much on the teleprompter came on St. Patrick's Day in 2009 when Brian Cowen, the Taoiseach (Prime Minister) of Ireland, visited the White House.

After a brief introduction by President Barack Obama, Mr. Cowen came to the podium. He read from the teleprompter "wing screens" for about 20 seconds before realizing he was reading words prepared not for him but for Mr. Obama. The teleprompter operator had been slow to switch scripts.

A little dismayed jocularity followed, and then Mr. Obama stepped to the podium. He started reading from the teleprompter, but now the script had belatedly been switched to Mr. Cowen's prepared text. So Mr. Obama proceeded to thank himself ("First, I'd like to say thank you to President Obama...") for coming to the White House.

There's a lesson here: Don't get lazy about the thoughts you're conveying. Keep your brain in gear. Know your material backward and forward.

REHEARSAL TIPS

Murphy—the one in Murphy's Law—delights in sabotaging the unprepared. It's all well and good to have a well-crafted script or a teleprompter setup or extensive notes; it's fine to have staging professionals and communications staff on hand. But none of that takes the place of knowing your content inside and out, and being prepared for Mr. Murphy. To help you get to that point, we offer the following tips:

1 Round up a rehearsal audience—even a few people will do—to hear and comment on your run-through. They could be your office mates, your admin staff, your spouse. But have at least one person there who won't be afraid to tell you the truth.

2 Rehearse even if you can't corral any victims, because the rehearsal itself remains top priority. Do it aloud, of course, preferably in surroundings approximating as closely as possible the actual venue. Bill Lane, the long-time speechwriter for former GE boss Jack Welch, favors the company auditorium. Nice if you have one, but don't let it stop you if you don't. Lane, incidentally, describes what you can expect once you clear your throat: "For the first few minutes this approach will be surreal—the sound of your voice in the empty room analogous to the tree falling in the empty forest. But drive on and in a few minutes you will get the same buzz as if there were a hundred people in front of you. Suddenly digressions will become apparent, boring passages, unnecessary discussion, rambling, and non sequiturs will ooze out, if there are any. And there will be. You may stand there experiencing the unusual phenomenon of boring yourself. These passages must be hacked out of your pitch after you finish rehearsing."[1]

3 Aim for at least two rehearsal sessions, not just one, and not just the night before. Your brain will use the rest period(s) well because you'll continue to think about the pitch and what you should adjust next.

4 In the later stages of rehearsal (after you've cut out the seriously boring stuff), turn on a video recorder. When you watch the result (trust us, you won't like it), ask yourself: Was your delivery dull? Did you merely read, or were you conversational and animated? Was your voice strong and energetic throughout? Remember: This is live theater you're engaged in. The volume and tone of your delivery may sound fine to your own ear, but to an audience of any considerable size, it probably will sound flat. Work on that. When it sounds to you like you're being overly dramatic, even ridiculously dramatic, it's probably about right.

5 If you're using PowerPoint, get familiar with the black-out key (the "b" when you're in Slide-Show view). This lets you kill the

[1] Bill Lane, *Jacked Up*, p. 234

visual distraction if you're interrupted with a question or if the slide loses relevance to the next part of your talk. (P.S., there's also a white-out key, which is the "w" when you're in Slide-Show view.)

> **"If you haven't rehearsed carefully and often, you're susceptible to booby traps."**

6 If your script will ultimately reside on a teleprompter, be sure to have at least two complete run-throughs with the actual device. Get acquainted with the teleprompter operator; he or she is now your best friend. See our sidebar, "A Tricky Friend".

7 As with a hard-copy script, your goal with a teleprompter is to "glance and grab" each phrase, shift eye contact to the audience, and glance and grab again.

8 Be sure to move your head and body naturally as you switch your gaze from one screen to the other. It doesn't look good if your head is motionless while only your eyes flit back and forth. Looking shifty is what that's called.

A sure-fire way to bore an audience is to "talk to" a succession of slides. "We groan," said a veteran of the presentation wars, "when we have to attend a meeting with the slide deck as the star." The problem was put succinctly in a cartoon in *The New Yorker* magazine, in which Satan is sitting behind a big desk in his office in Hell and he's talking to an underling: "I need someone well versed in the art of torture," he says. "Do you know PowerPoint?" PowerPoint might not in fact be a torture device. It might not be downright evil, as Yale professor Edward Tufte suggests it is. But as a weapon for persuasion, it is unquestionably a dud. Why?

1 Charts are lousy at telling a story. And the best attack vehicle for making a presentation is a story. It is not a laundry list of talking points. (More on that below.)

2 A bulleted list of talking points makes it difficult to distinguish the important from the unimportant. That weakness is illustrated by the PowerPoint deck that NASA put together for some critical meetings in January 2003. They were trying to assess the risks of going ahead as scheduled with the reentry of the space shuttle Columbia. They decided to go ahead, and the reentry attempt, on February 1, destroyed the craft and killed everyone on board. A post-disaster study commission suggested that the catastrophe might have been averted if, instead of bulleted charts, mission controllers had had a full, narrative description of the situation they were facing. One crucial technical detail never got much consideration in the decision to go ahead with the reentry as planned. Unfortunately, it was buried as a cryptic sub-sub-bullet item at the bottom of one chart in the middle of a large deck. With no narrative that spelled out the potential impact of that detail, it's no wonder they missed it.

3 Chart language typically consists of incomplete thoughts or meaningless fragments. The connective tissues that might persuade the listener to buy into the speaker's position—the transitions, explanations, elaborations—are missing. You're relying on a source that's basically incoherent.

4 Charts can destroy the attention that should be focused on you and your words. The human mind doesn't do well processing multiple sources of information at the same time. *You* are supposed to be the source of information. So a chart is either a distraction from what *you* are saying, or *you* are the distraction, distracting those who are trying to decipher a chart.

Not that PowerPoint doesn't have its uses. It does. However, for a serious attempt at persuasion, for confirming, challenging, or changing the emotions, beliefs, or ideas of your audience, slide software must be used sparingly, if at all. The slides do not make a presentation. *You* do. It is you, not the slides, who must grab and hold the audience's attention and make the case.

THE STORY'S THE THING

How do you do that? Answer: You think story. "Story" means a narrative that stimulates basic human interest or emotions and draws people into your message. It means connecting with your audience at a gut level. But how do you develop a story? It's really a simple, two-step process.

First, make it personal. Think of something that has happened in your life that can be related to the message of your talk. Something about yourself or your kids, your spouse or your uncle, a friend, a colleague, anybody you know. If it's about some failure or misstep on your part— some doubt or fear or confusion—so much the better. Audiences like to be assured that you are one of them, a normal, fallible human being. Once so assured, they'll be vastly more receptive to what you say next.

The "tell-a-story" idea may sound corny when you're setting out to make a major presentation about company strategy or quarterly earnings. But there's no event or circumstance that doesn't have a story behind it. Maybe some of the "team" did better than expected because they tried harder and made a real breakthrough. That's a story. Even a complex corporate strategy has story elements; they just have to be recognized and developed.

The second step in developing a story is to organize your presentation in writing. A written narrative forces you to think through the logic and persuasiveness of your argument. It enables you to spot flaws and weaknesses, and to correct them, before the audience gets its shot.

It's not until you are well into this process of building a story that you should be thinking about what charts and visuals might be used to reinforce or punctuate your main points. Reinforcing, punctuating: that is their proper role. And whatever visuals you choose, make sure they have impact, like big animal pictures, or cartoons and the like. The smallest number of accompanying words possible is best.

Now you refine and rehearse the narrative aloud until you've got it internalized. Internalized means you've mastered the thrust of what you want to say. It does not mean memorized. Don't worry if you find yourself unconsciously straying from the exact words and phrasing of the script.

That said, there are certain occasions when you may have to, like it or not, stick as closely as possible to the script. Testimony before a legislative committee, for example. Or earnings commentary before stockholders and investment analysts, where every word will be weighed and every sentence dissected. But for most other occasions, the essential thing is not the precision with which you read a script but the conviction and energy with which you convey the message.

Once comfortable with the flow, the logic, and the messaging, you may then use the full script for your support at the podium or on the teleprompter. Or you can shrink it down to a set of notes or talking points, shrinking it to whatever level works for you. Remember, though, whether you use full text or notes, you want the audience focused primarily on you and your ideas.

Once you've made a shorter, talking-points version of your pitch, rehearse the shorter version. Invariably, at this point, you'll find yourself stumbling and fumbling as you go from one point to the next because the transitions won't be spelled out for you. This is precisely why you're rehearsing.

Is this hard? You bet it is. But no pain, as they say, no gain. Or as a GE major domo advised Bill Lane to tell other GE executives: "Tell them they are going nowhere in the General Electric Company if they can't do a great business presentation."

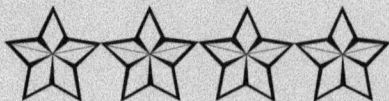

GEORGE S. PATTON, JR.

If somebody asked you to name great orators of the World War II period, you might easily mention Franklin Delano Roosevelt and Winston Churchill. Most likely, that would be it. (If you wanted to raise some eyebrows you might mention Adolf Hitler. Der Führer was certainly a remarkable orator, but we'll just sidestep that one anyway.) But apart from these well-known statesmen, some of the most noted orators of the Second World War were soldiers. One in particular was "Old Blood and Guts," General George S. Patton, Jr.

The American press gave him that nickname. Why? Well, here he is in one little speech[2] to the troops on the eve of the Normandy invasion: "We're not going to just shoot the sons-of-bitches, we're going to rip out their living goddamned guts and use them to grease the treads of our tanks." Any more questions?

Sentiments like those might have sounded a little funny coming from a man whose voice was into the upper register, as Patton's was. Not quite Pee Wee Hermanish, but definitely high pitched. And he did feel self-conscious about it. But that didn't stop him doing what he thought was essential to get the job done. Leaders, wrote Patton[3], "must make it a point to be physically seen by as many individuals of their command as possible.... The best way to do this is to assemble the divisions, either as a whole or in separate pieces, and make a short talk."

[2] Per Richard Sassaman in *America in WWII magazine*, April 2010
[3] In a piece titled "War as I Knew It", per Sassaman, ibid.

Patton gave many small talks, and each was usually very well rehearsed. His practice would include standing in front of a mirror and putting on his "war face"—partly, perhaps, to compensate for his high-pitched voice. He knew that when you endeavor to make a presentation, you are—like it or not—entering the special realm of show business. In a cover story two months before Normandy, *Time* magazine wrote that "Patton the General is also Patton the Actor: Showmanship is instinctive in him." And years earlier, Patton himself wrote[4] that "The leader must be an actor... He is unconvincing unless he lives his part."

Does this mean the giver of a presentation, the speaker, must become a phony in order to succeed? If your words—like those of the classic snake-oil salesman—are intended to misinform or mislead, the answer is yes. But creating an atmosphere that stimulates interest in what you are saying is not being a phony. Showmanship is about injecting personality, temperament, and emotion into a pitch. It's about "softening up the battlefield" so the audience is thinking about you and your message and not other things; it's about making a connection with other human beings, about not seeming bored by having to say whatever it is you're saying.

For Patton, leadership "was never simply about making plans and giving orders," writes Alan Axelrod in his book *Patton: A Biography* (2006)[5]. "It was about transforming oneself into a symbol, a kind of totem or talisman with which the group identified. His message was never *we must succeed* but always *we will succeed*."

To go with his "war face," there were words. And the words Patton chose were those that he calculated would resonate most strongly with his audience. Here is how he ended another speech to his troops preparing to invade Normandy: "There is one great thing you men will all be able to say when you go home. You may thank God for it. Thank God, that at least, thirty years from now, when you are sitting around the fireside with your grandson on your knees, and he asks you what

[4]In *The Secret of Victory* (1926), per Sassaman, ibid.
[5]In a piece titled "War as I Knew It", per Sassaman, ibid.

you did in the Great War, you won't have to cough and say, 'I shoveled shit in Louisiana.'"

Patton liked to project an image that was not that of a man of arts and letters. Ironically, though, he was the "most widely read general in the American army," according to military historian Victor Davis Hanson[6]. He was the quintessential man of action, a persona that showed up in his vivid way with words.

His words, his style, reflected his training as a cavalry officer before World War I. In that tradition, success went to quick decision and speed in execution—better a good plan executed now than a perfect plan next week. He believed that a continual forward motion, in both word and deed, had two effects: It demoralized the enemy and it energized oneself.

For a speechmaker, this means eschewing elaborate prose. "You are here to fight," he told an assembly of his large headquarters staff when he took over command of the Third Army in early 1944. "This is an active theater of war. Ahead of you lies battle. That means just one thing. You can't afford to be a goddamned fool, because, in battle, fools mean dead men." No elaborate prose there.

Patton's Achilles' heel was his lack of PR sense. He "never understood [the] rhetorical responsibilities of a public figure," writes Victor Davis Hanson.[7] Thus, while military censors strove to keep images of death out of the American media, Patton in a Memorial Day speech in 1943 said this: "To conquer, we must destroy our enemies.... We must kill devastatingly. The faster and more effectively you kill, the longer you will live to enjoy the priceless fame of conquerors." One can just imagine the effect of such prose on any delicate sensibilities; the censors must have had heart attacks.

Not all such slips were Patton's fault, however. At the opening ceremonies of a Welcome Club for soldiers near the village of Knutsford, England, shortly before the Normandy invasion, he was

[6-7]Per Sassaman, ibid.

called upon to make a few extemporaneous remarks. One of his remarks was, "It is the evident destiny of the British and Americans, and, of course, the Russians, to rule the world..." Newspapers on both sides of the Atlantic, however, omitted his mention of Russia, which was then an ally of the Western powers, and the faulty reports landed him in hot water.

It was also the lack of preparation that led to the faux pas. Extemporizing is always a risky affair for someone in a high-profile occupation.

CHAPTER FIVE:
LAUNCH THE ATTACK.

"I determined to do on the 23rd what had been intended to be done on the 24th... Sherman's command was in position, though one division had not yet crossed the river... but I was determined to move that night even without this division."

— GEN. ULYSSES S. GRANT,
*on launching the attack at the
Battle of Chattanooga, 1863*

CHAPTER FIVE:
LAUNCH
THE ATTACK.

LET THEM KNOW YOU ARE GOING TO WIN.

Your first tactical objective in any executive presentation is to capture as many members of the audience as possible. More precisely, to capture the audience's attention.

The obstacles are many, but your most dangerous enemy is time. You have not minutes but only seconds to persuade your audience that what you have to say is worthy of their attention. Start strong. Timidity never won a skirmish, let alone a war. This holds true for both the Surprise Attack and the Soften-up-the-Battlefield presentation structure.

Don't stint on formulating your attack; spend as much time as necessary on the opening salvo. Should it be based on whimsy? Shock and awe? Surprise? Or perhaps candor? An example of the latter is seen in a talk that Frank Shrontz, then-president of the Boeing Company, gave to a group of Pentagon officials back in the 1980s. That was after reports had surfaced of major defense contractors grossly overcharging the government for ordinary items— there was, for example, the infamous $700 toilet seat. Here was Shrontz's opening:

> We, and here I mean both our industry in general and my
> company in particular, have done some dumb things.[8]

That statement may not seem strong at first, but it is. It is riveting. Disarming. Using candor and the plainest language, Shrontz immediately made some captures. In battlefield terminology, this

---

[8] Jeff Scott Cook, *The Elements of Speechwriting and Public Speaking*, p. 192

> **"It is you, not the slides, who must grab and hold the audience's attention and make the case."**

would be called a feint, a maneuver to draw the enemy toward you or toward a predetermined point. If this were hand-to-hand combat, it's the equivalent of judo—literally the "gentle way," turning your opponent's own energy against him. The opponent's energy in this case was the pent-up umbrage of the Pentagon officials. They had been mightily embarrassed by the bad publicity and were ready to lambast this big defense contractor if they had heard any hint of justification for the overcharges.

But whatever your choice of opening, you must refine and refine, then rehearse and rehearse.

And what about the message itself? Here your enemies are more numerous.

One is your organizational bureaucracy. The danger is the habit of seeking input from all your internal and external constituents. The result can be the dreaded laundry list. Or the freight train, as some people call it: a slow, endless, procession of railroad cars, clickety-clack, clickety-clack, each with a different cargo. Most of your captives will be over the wall before you're halfway through.

A second enemy is the temptation to tell everything you know about a given subject. In talking about everything, you leave the audience with nothing in particular to remember.

A third enemy is prose that beats around the bush and never gets to the point. If you want to deliver a message, damn it! (as Patton would say), deliver the message. Or as Admiral Nelson instructed his captains, "Never mind about maneuvers, go straight at 'em." Nelson's command applies even to the little matter (it's actually a big matter) of sentence construction and tempo.

See, for example, if you can spot a certain pattern in the sentences that follow; they come from a white paper on software technology and are the lead-off sentences in the first several paragraphs:

> *"Although delivering software as a subscription service got off to a very rocky start, both the market and the industry have since developed a solid foundation..."*

> *"Although the hosting of traditional packaged applications has jumped off to the fastest start, net-native software-as-services (SaS) applications are gaining a great deal of traction..."*

> *"Although these plans span all company sizes and industries, small (under 100 employees) and mid-market companies (those with between 100 and 1,000 employees) have a particular affinity to this new class of application..."*

Exactly. Each sentence starts with a lengthy clause denoted by "although." That leading clause is intended to qualify the main point, which comes only later in the clause that follows the comma. The effect is deadly (in a manner of speaking). But the author is still not finished with us. In several more paragraphs, he apparently recognizes the monotonous repetition, but he thinks the problem is fixed if he switches from "although" to "while" a couple of times. So the next few paragraphs begin thusly:

> *"While services-based delivery still accounts for only about 6.5% of the $84 billion application software market, it is by far the most rapidly growing segment..."*

"While virtually all application ISVs will have to increasingly offer their software as a service, this does not mean they must, or even should own all the capabilities required to do so..."

"While a large number of companies are willing and able to provide some of these skills, precious few are capable of taking single-source responsibility for these functions."

See the problem? It's not the first word. It's that business of beginning each sentence with a long-winded qualification of what you're about to say. And a reader or listener can't keep all that qualifying stuff in mind when you finally get around to the main point. On a larger scale ("Everything depends on the scale of events," said Churchill.), danger lurks in feeling obligated to observe certain conventions during a formal speech: conventions such as thanking the host for the introduction, or recognizing various and sundry personages on the dais. We're not saying don't observe the conventions, but do keep them short.

NAPOLEON'S WAY WITH WORDS

WANT TO BE BRIEF AND TO THE POINT? LET NAPOLEON BE YOUR GUIDE.

It's doubtful that anyone who heard "the Little Corporal" give one of his speeches or read one of his postings (posted, literally, on trees in those days) ever wondered what he was getting at. It was not his style to indulge in the fancy circumlocutions that were fashionable in that period. In all his communications he was determined to be well understood, even to the most common foot soldier. He did not preface his pronouncements with, "Let me be clear...," as if someone was trying to stop him. He *was* clear. Here is the start of his proclamation to his soldiers on entering Milan, Italy, on the 15th of May, 1796:

> *Soldiers: You have rushed like a torrent from the top of the Apennines; you have overthrown and scattered all that opposed your march. Piedmont, delivered from Austrian tyranny, indulges her natural sentiments of peace and friendship toward France. Milan is yours, and the Republican flag waves throughout Lombardy. The Dukes of Parma and Modena owe their political existence to your generosity alone. The army which so proudly threatened you can find no barrier to protect it against your courage; neither the Po, the Ticino, nor the Adda [rivers] could stop you for a single day.*

No wonder his troops were so loyal to him. So loyal, in fact, that after he was first dethroned and exiled to Elba, he had no trouble gathering those same troops around him when he escaped and reappeared on the French coast ten months later. What actually happened was the court of King Louis XVIII sent a regiment to intercept Napoleon when they heard what was up. Napoleon, moving up from the coast on horseback and accompanied by a small retinue, spotted the king's men just south of Grenoble, whereupon he dismounted and, leaving his retinue behind, approached the soldiers on foot until he was within gunshot range. He shouted, "Here I am. Kill your emperor, if you wish." The soldiers responded with, "Vive L'Empereur!" and marched with Napoleon toward Paris, from which place the king, having taken stock of the fresh circumstances, decided to absent himself.

Before he met his Waterloo a year later, however, you didn't want to be on the wrong end of certain of Napoleon's presentations. Here he is in 1796, still in Italy, during the siege of Mantua:

> *Soldiers: I am not satisfied with you. You have shown neither bravery, discipline, nor perseverance. No position could rally you. You abandoned yourselves to a panic-terror. You suffered yourselves to be driven from situations where a handful of brave men might have stopped an army. Soldiers of the 39th and 85th, you are not French soldiers. Quartermaster-general, let it be inscribed on their colors, "They no longer form part of the Army of Italy!"*

NAPOLEON COULD STAB YOU WITH WORDS

A hundred years later, the Progressive-era journalist Ira Tarbell wrote that Napoleon "used words almost as effectively as the sword, and that, throughout his career, the [speech or presentation] ably supported the military maneuver..."

In March of 1797, at the end of his first campaign against the principalities of Italy, Napoleon's troops were hungry and exhausted, and not especially eager to launch themselves into yet another campaign. So Napoleon's first goal was to boost their spirits:

> Soldiers: The campaign just ended has given you imperishable renown. You have been victorious in fourteen pitched battles and seventy actions. You have taken more than a hundred thousand prisoners, five hundred field-pieces, two thousand heavy guns, and four pontoon trains.

Note the quick recitation of numbers and facts to support that claim of "renown." Point proven. He goes on:

> In addition to this, you have sent six millions to the public treasury, and have enriched the National Museum with three hundred masterpieces of the arts of ancient and modern Italy, which it has required thirty centuries to produce. [The Italians could not have been too thrilled about this, but remember, his audience was his French troops.] You have conquered the finest countries in Europe. The French flag waves for the first time upon the Adriatic opposite to Macedon, the native country of Alexander [the Great].

Wow! Cool. Okay, we may wonder if the poor common foot soldier was so thrilled at the prospect of the Mona Lisa hanging in the Louvre, since he probably never heard of either the Mona Lisa or the Louvre. And yet, quibbles aside, we may presume that Napoleon knew his men and knew how to buck them up, to swell their pride. But now came the tricky part: To rouse them from their desperately needed rest and into another hard slog. So he pivots with a promise of further glory:

> Still higher destinies await you. I know that you will not prove unworthy of them. Of all the foes that conspired to stifle the Republic [of France] in its birth, the Austrian Emperor alone remains before you.

"Right," groans the cynical foot soldier. "The Austrian Emperor alone? You mean him and the Alps and a hundred thousand troops we have to get through first."

But never mind. Napoleon concludes with a warning. A clear but subtle warning about any unnecessary roughness in the soon-to-be conquered lands:

> You will there find a brave people, whose religion and customs you will respect, and whose prosperity you will hold sacred. Remember that it is liberty you carry to the brave Hungarian nation. (Hungary was part of the Austrian Empire at that time.)

Nothing oblique, round-about, or wishy-washy is found in Bonaparte's style. The passive voice is unknown to him. He shares with many other great leaders a passion for clarity, simplicity, and directness—a determination that his message should not be lost or misunderstood.

CHAPTER SIX:
TAKE CAPTIVES AND INSPIRE THEM TO JOIN YOU.

"I am very anxious that any great disaster, or the capture of our men in great numbers, shall be avoided."

- ABRAHAM LINCOLN TO GEN. ULYSSES S GRANT,
April 1864

CHAPTER SIX:
TAKE CAPTIVES AND INSPIRE THEM TO JOIN YOU.

THE PRESENTER AS LEADER.

Camille Lavington, an executive career counselor in New York, wrote a book with the title, *You've Only Got Three Seconds.* Her thesis is that when you walk into a roomful of strangers, it takes people all of about three seconds to look you over and size you up—to know where you're coming from.

Lucky for you, in a presentation situation you have more than three seconds to make an impression. But that's only because of a few necessary civilities, such as thanking your host for the introduction or acknowledging others who may be sharing the dais with you. With all that, you may have a whole minute. But don't push it. Many speakers waste this critical time with overly long tributes to the host, to the audience, to the event producers, and others. Worse yet, they try to tell a joke. Bad move when the immediate need is *capture*—the capture of attention. Audiences today are sophisticated products of a supersaturated media world in which thousands of messages each day are aimed at grabbing their attention. Those messages must quickly hit their mark or they'll miss entirely. Same goes for you.

As the rawest infantry recruit will know, surprise is generally the first weapon of choice in making a capture. This form of attack is often best launched, unsurprisingly, in silence. (This opening tactic applies to both types of presentation: Surprise Attack and Soften-Up-the-Battlefield Preparation.)

Silence? What do we mean? Try this: When you step onto the stage or behind the podium, say nothing at all for a moment, except perhaps for the obligatory "Thank you" to whoever introduced you. Stand there for a moment. If at a podium, lay out your notes or the script. Take a deep breath, let it out slowly, and relax, at the same time looking congenially into the faces of individual audience members. Soak up the expressions, be they good, bad, or indifferent. Take a good look again. Smile.

What you're doing is beating them to the punch in the sizing-up game. The first surprise for these soon-to-be captives is the absence of any vocalisms coming from you. You're supposed to be saying something and you're not. You're creating rising expectation and mystery. "Hmm," they wonder, "what's he thinking about? He looks so confident."

We're not talking about an uncomfortable span of time. Five or ten seconds can be more than enough. But those early seconds can be salutary all around. You the speaker are indulging in an excellent remedy for nervousness, and you've captured attention, without a word yet spoken.

NOW, BEGIN.

Your objective is to secure the captives and prevent escapes. But caution: You can't do this well if you are fussing and fidgeting with props or equipment or PCs — anything. All that has to be done ahead of time. When you take the stage, you take command.

Avoiding self-sabotage is key. Self-sabotage can take the form of a number of personal nervous tics—verbal ones like *uhs*, *ums*, and *you knows*, or physical ones like your eyes fastened on the back wall instead of on the audience. If the audience is zeroing-in on such tics, they're not hearing your message. Escapes are imminent. Don't put your hands in your pocket. Don't fuss with your cell phone or Blackberry, and don't carry a cup of coffee or a bottle of water around.

Your audience didn't come to watch you drink coffee or see what kind of bottled water you drink.

If there's room to move around the stage, do so. "Working the room" means moving from one spot on the stage to another, addressing particular sections of the audience. But don't move continuously; it's distracting. Having stepped to a new spot, plant your feet for a moment and complete the point you're making before taking another step.

Do, on the other hand, use your hands. Hands and arms, as basic to human expression as the voice, bring visible impact into the battle for attention. Go with the energy that your hands will naturally convey if you let them. But don't force it, don't plan your gestures, don't be robotic. Let your hands do what they naturally do when you're making a point or telling a story. Practice in front of a mirror. But practice what?

That brings us to our next topic: The script.

YOUR BATTLE EQUIPMENT

There's a curious thing about full-text narrative scripts. Not about the scripts, actually, but about many executives and power players who think they shouldn't be seen reading their words. To them it feels awkward. They dread the prospect of sounding stilted, plodding, droning. This is part of the driving force behind the PowerPoint plague. Many presenters feel more comfortable putting crib notes on a sequence of slides that they can then "talk to." (For our fuller take on the PowerPoint Syndrome, see "The Biggest Crutch" on page 48.) The audience, in effect, is slighted; they're ignored in favor of a slide screen.

Many executives also love using a teleprompter, but usually for the wrong reason.

> *"This is a godsend. I can look like I'm looking straight at*

the audience and deliver every word of the script my staff
prepared for me, and the silly old audience will never be the
wiser. Right? I don't have to spend so much of my valuable time
practicing. Right? It's all good."

Forget it. Only the most sheltered of waifs might think that someone making any kind of scheduled presentation is extemporizing.

We all knew—didn't we?—exactly what President Obama was doing when he gazed left in a speech, then switched his gaze 90 degrees to his right. We all knew those angled gizmos he was looking at (they're called "wing screens") were not some equipment left behind by the janitorial crew.

To a certain extent, audiences do appreciate those little contrivances that help camouflage the speaker's use of a script or notes. And for you, the speaker, those contrivances help you make better eye contact and thus better audience connections. Audiences like that, yes, but what they like even more is an interesting, logical flow of thought. No meandering, off-topic half-thoughts, no nervous verbal tics that make them wonder: "Where's this guy going? Why didn't he think enough of us to do the work of organizing his thoughts?"

Your job is not to spurn a script. Your job is to get good at using one. It is to get good at whatever support tools will suit your style and purpose, whether a full-blown script scrolling on a teleprompter, or a printed text lying on the podium, or notes held in your hand, or bullet points on a screen. (Yes, even PowerPoint has its uses.)

But keep this in mind: As IT industry thought leader Tom Hickman likes to say: "Don't be afraid to edit if the flow is off, or if the transitions are awkward. Strive for perfection, because you—not your tech writer, not your communications director, not your Marketing and Communications temp—are giving the presentation."

This takes time. And effort. In the middle of fighting World War II,

Winston Churchill would labor for days in preparing for a ten-minute speech. Steve Jobs typically spent several days rehearsing on *stage* before doing one of his legendary new-product pitches. In all such cases the *preparation* included building a full-blown written narrative of what the speaker wanted to say, followed by repeated practice and revision, practice and revision, practice and revision.

Victory doesn't come without preparation.

KEEP IT SIMPLE

Communicating aurally is vastly different than communicating in print. That's because the ear—as one sage put it—is one-tenth the organ of the eye. Never forget that. It's the most powerful of all insights into the making of a successful presentation The point is that when you're reading printed information, you can always go back and reread what you don't immediately understand. You can set your own pace in assimilating the words and ideas coming at you. You can linger, you can savor, you can pause and reflect before moving on. If you are the writer, you have the luxury of being able to capitalize on that fact by cramming lots of facts and ideas into a sentence; you can festoon the sentence with parenthetic phrases and subordinate clauses. You can load a ton of data into a chart. The reader may not like having to work so hard to grasp your meaning, but if the content is important enough to him, written communication does give him the means to absorb every bit of it.

Not so a live speech. There's no pause button or rewind button. The ear demands to be spoon fed. One fact at a time, one idea at a time. This brings us to a cardinal rule of thumb if you want to be readily understood: Stick to simple declarative sentences.

A perfect example comes from Bill O'Reilly, the Fox News personality. Here he is giving a commencement address to an audience of high-school graduates: "There is an order to your life. You will succeed unless you screw it up. Your parents and teachers have provided most of you with the opportunity to build a foundation. You can do what I have done. You can go beyond what I have done. Be honorable. Find your talent. Work hard. And be true to yourself. Your life is waiting for you."

O'Reilly understands that the ear is one-tenth the organ of the eye. But he's hardly the first to figure that out. Just dip into one of Shakespeare's plays, for example—all written for the ear. He repeated key words and phrases two and three times, sometimes using the same word in a different sense to stress his point and create a compelling rhythm and timing.

This points again to the necessity of practicing and rehearsing. Practicing your presentation aloud, in full voice, will uncover the awkward sections, where rhythm, timing, and sequence need to be improved. Great presenters generally have a great rhythm. Great rhythm comes from practice—a lot of practice.

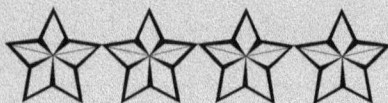

WINSTON CHURCHILL
'STUPID' BOY MAKES GOOD

"THAT WHICH DOES NOT KILL ME MAKES ME STRONGER."

So said Friedrich Nietzsche. And so might anyone say who undertakes to make a public presentation. Winston Churchill might have muttered something very similar at various points in his life. In fact, as a youthful, battle-seasoned cavalry officer, Churchill wrote that "Nothing in life is more exhilarating as to be shot at without result." Later in life, as a politician and statesman, Churchill knew what it was like to be shot at, metaphorically speaking, in his presentations.

Churchill today is mostly, if not solely, remembered for his leadership as the British prime minister during World War II. Less well known is that, by the time he took on the premiership, he had already spent 40 years in and out of government. They were tumultuous years, including a stint as First Lord of the Admiralty during World War I. At the start of World War II he was 65 years old and, up until the moment he took over, he was widely considered all washed up. A has-been. True, he was already immensely accomplished: military leader, political leader, journalist, historian. (He was later to be awarded a Nobel Prize in Literature.) But as the 1930s rolled along, he was widely seen as having created too many enemies and burned too many bridges.

His leadership in the war against Hitler took many forms, but none was more prominent than the brilliance of his speechwriting and speechmaking. This was foretold even in his boyhood days at Harrow (the equivalent of a private high school in the United States). He was considered the "stupidest boy in the school," according to one of his biographers. Yet he often ghostwrote essays for classmates who had difficulty writing.

His first book, published just before the turn of the century, won widespread acclaim. It was an account of battles between British forces, which included himself, and Pashtun tribesmen along what was then the India-Afghanistan frontier (what is now Pakistan) in 1897. The acclaim astonished him. "I had never been praised before," he wrote. "The only comments which had ever been made upon my work at school had been 'Indifferent,' 'Untidy,' 'Slovenly,' 'Bad,' 'Very bad,' etc."

That acclaim, plus his later exploits in the Boer War, won him a seat in Parliament. It's at this stage that the early Churchill gives us (as he gave himself) some sharp lessons in making a presentation. As was true for the rest of his career, his speeches were marked by meticulous preparation. He virtually memorized every word, every sentence— even every gesture he planned to make. Before each speech, and apart from the writing, he would practice for many hours in front of a mirror. It worked, for the most part, and it was quickly forgotten that he had a lisp. (Yes, one of the greatest speakers of all time had a speech impediment.)

It worked, that is, until April 22, 1904, when disaster struck. Elsewhere in this book we warn against attempting to rely exclusively on one's memory in preparing for a presentation. And Churchill, who had a phenomenal memory, shows us why. For his first few years in Parliament, he operated as though his memory would never fail him, referring to no texts, or even notes, as he spoke. But then came that day when he was reaching the peroration of a long speech. Here's how his great biographer William Manchester described it:

> *He was speaking with his customary fire, and was about to strike his right fist into his left palm, clinching his argument, when his mind went completely blank. He had just said: "It lies with the Government to satisfy the working classes that there is no justification...." His voice trailed off. He groped. The studied phrases, laboriously composed and learned by heart, had fled from his memory. He began again: "It lies with them ....What?" he asked, as though someone had suggested a cue. He hesitated, frowned, looked confused, and fumbled in the pockets of his frock coat, as though looking for notes. There were none; until now he hadn't carried any. The MP beside him picked some paper scraps from the floor; there was nothing on them. Winston made one more try: "It lies with them to satisfy the electors..." Some members cheered encouragingly, but it was no good. He sat down abruptly, buried his face in his hands, and muttered: "I thank the honorable members for having listened to me."*

Another biographer, Roy Jenkins, more recently put it this way: "His internal teleprompter suddenly collapsed." But the lesson was learned. He subsequently carried the text of the speech with him at every formal presentation, even though he seldom needed it.

Something else we can emulate about Churchill is his fondness for words that packed a punch. His vocabulary was enormous, but the words he favored most were the simplest and shortest. Just before the entrance of America into World War II, Britain was alone in facing off against Hitler. He didn't ask the U.S. for military equipment so the Brits "could mount an adequate defense." Instead he said, "Give us the tools and we will finish the job." He didn't say, as Roy Jenkins put it, "that the Allies had 'consented to a coalition' or 'agreed to cooperate.' Instead, they had 'joined hands.'"

Churchill hated jargon. In one session of Parliament, an MP had littered his presentation with it, and Churchill later commented: "He can best be described as one of those orators who, before they get up, do not know what they are going to say; when they are speaking, do not know what they are saying; and when they have sat down, do not know what they have said."

Without question, it was Churchill's early acquaintance with the battlefield that fed and reinforced his power as a speechmaker. At the same time, his way with words also influenced his wartime leadership. General Montgomery, for example, once resisted Churchill's admonition that the general ought to study logistics, saying he shouldn't become involved in such technical matters. "After all, you know, they say that familiarity breeds contempt." At this, Churchill replied: "I would like to remind you that without a degree of familiarity we could not breed anything."

CHAPTER SEVEN:
COMMIT RESERVES IF NEEDED.

"In war the will is directed at an animate object that reacts."

- CARL VON CLAUSEWITZ

CHAPTER SEVEN:
COMMIT RESERVES
IF NEEDED.

POUNCE AT THE CRITICAL POINT AND TIME.

Well done so far. You've acquired a camcorder or at least a voice recorder, and several times you've gone through your script *aloud*, making tweaks and improvements at each iteration. (Did we say *aloud*? Yes we did.)

You've got the trajectory of the argument, along with the theme, to the point that you can comfortably take your eyes off the script or the teleprompter and fasten them on individual members of the audience. You're able now to finish the thought before you return your eyes to the script or teleprompter to pick up the next thought. You know that this is not reading but *performing*, and that therefore you must bring extra energy and conviction into your voice and body language. You're also learning to pause and go silent for a moment rather than emit an *um*, *uh*, or *you know*. You appreciate, as you play back your recording, that the pauses are infinitely nicer than the verbal tics.

All good. But, what if you also know that this will be a contentious audience, maybe a skeptical, suspicious, argumentative one? To handle this, you can be one of two things: preemptive or reactive. Or both. In any case, you will be marshalling your reserve forces.

Let's take preemption first. Here, an effective way to deploy your reserves is by mandating the use of footnoting during the scripting process. But wait, you're probably thinking: This sounds way too tweedy and academic for a hard-charging leader. Be that as it may, if you see any signs of skepticism in the audience as you're speaking (e.g., smirks, raised eyebrows, shaking heads), those little notes at the bottom of your script pages can be the grenades you'll want to lob into the sniper's nest. Before the drafting process begins, issue an order to your speechwriter or researcher to footnote the sources for any data or quotes or other factual information you may use.

> **"Those little footnotes at the bottom of your script pages can be the grenades you'll want to lob into the sniper's nest."**

For obvious reasons, though, footnoting doesn't work well with a teleprompter. In those cases, you want to arrange to have a confederate sitting in the front row, armed with the footnoted script. If smirks appear, you can ad lib something like this: "Now I know some of you may be skeptical about what I'm saying, but it comes from a reliable source. And I think Mike has that exact information handy, don't you Mike? Mike is our CFO." Mike in the front row thereupon pipes up with chapter and verse.

It's possible to have footnotes built into your teleprompter script—color-coded or set off in such way that it's clear you're not to refer to it unless necessary. This approach is tricky, however, and depends on close work with the teleprompter operator.

Another idea is to have a hard copy of the book or magazine that's a key source in your talk stashed away on the podium, ready to bring out and hold up for the audience's gaze. Props are good. These ploys are preemptive.

On the *reactive* side, the place to deploy your reserves is during the Q&A.

Say you just finished your speech and the cheers weren't exactly deafening. You've now opened the floor to questions and you can easily make out a dozen sharpshooters drawing a bead on you.

As Roy Milligan, a longtime communications veteran with HP U.S., and now with Glass Beehive Communication LLC in Massachusetts, likes to say: "There are always people in the audience who like to have themselves heard. They can come in several varieties: Snipers, those with their own agenda who jump at targets of opportunity; Sharpshooters, those who let it be known that they know more than the presenter; and Gunners, people who like to hear their own voices."

Envisioning the moment when you will be standing before a live audience should have been as much a part of your preparation as the writing, drafting, and rehearsing of the speech itself.

You and your staff should have written down what you think are the hardest, bluntest, nastiest questions that might be asked. You should then have picked up this list and read the questions *aloud*. Then, along with your staffers and colleagues (especially your communications and PR support), you should have worked out answers that are

1 positive,

2 nondefensive, and

3 can be stated in ten seconds or less.

That time limit—ten seconds or less—is important because your goal is to reinforce points you just made in your presentation. You want to exploit the opening created by the question (regardless of what it was) to spend another 20 or 30 seconds reiterating one or more of the main positive message points that you made in the initial presentation.

Also important: Practice giving these answers with a smile. In the actual event, when the bullets fly, the first thing you must do is fight any temptation to look perturbed. Among the no-nos are crossing your arms, shaking your head, and putting your arms on your hips in a manner that might seem defiant.

"Never let 'em see you sweat" is always a good rule. Look directly at the questioner, nod that you understand the question, and again (assuming the occasion is not too dreadfully serious) smile. Adopt an open and friendly demeanor, being careful however not to seem smug or self-satisfied. This is not easy. But we can improve our ability to avoid getting angry by arming ourselves with honest and (one hopes) compelling answers to anticipated questions.

Have that footnoted script at the ready. Have that confederate in the front row. Have that book or magazine article handy to show, with the relevant parts highlighted.

Being ready with an extra video clip or two (beyond those that were part of the basic pitch) can also be effective in readying a counterattack. Your staff may well have come across a video clip that didn't quite fit the flow of your initial pitch, or was just one clip too many. Don't discard it. Have it cued up for an added shot here in the Q&A.

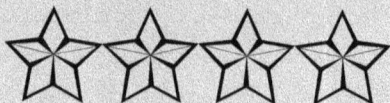

USAF COLONEL JOHN BOYD

A speaking engagement can be a dogfight—a head-to-head contest with your competitors. You may be part of a panel discussion at a big industry conference, for example, and other members of the panel include your archenemies in the marketplace. The challenge you face is to work the control stick, as it were, to put your company in a light more favorable than that in which your copanelists can put theirs.

Who better to turn to for advice, then, if not a battle-tested U.S. Air Force fighter pilot? That would be USAF Colonel John Boyd (1927-1997). It was Boyd who, after his combat service in the Korean War, developed the tactical theories that today are part of the training of fighter pilots of many of the world's air forces. More remarkable, though, is that Boyd's ideas are also taught in MBA classes at many top business schools. That's because commercial combat can get pretty serious. Ditto for certain presentation settings.

What Boyd did was come up with the concept of the OODA loop. Few people outside the military have heard of the OODA loop, and even fewer know what it stands for, but *inside* the military it resonates with almost mystical, Talmudic power. Inside *or* outside, this knowledge can serve speechmakers and presenters well.

So let's say you're on this panel, and you're only there because the colleague who was supposed to represent your company took ill. Plus, you have only a week's notice to prepare. Putting a rip-roaring presentation together in only a week's time may not seem like jet fighters in an aerial dogfight, but if you've been in that situation before, you know it's close.

OODA stands for Observe, Orient, Decide, and Act. Those are the four stages of mental and physical activity for anyone dealing with a rapidly unfolding sequence of events. And they work in a continuous cycle, or loop.

Colonel Boyd's colleagues had a nickname for him—"Forty-Second" Boyd. He came by that because, for a number of years following the Korean War, he had a standing bet with other fighter pilots. At 30,000 feet over a patch of Nevada desert, he would allow a challenger to get behind him in perfect shoot-down position. If, within 40 seconds—and with a $40 wager on the line—he was unable to turn the tables and get behind the challenger in position to shoot *him* down, the challenger would win. As far as we are aware, none did. By the time he retired in 1975, Boyd had refined and embellished his theory into a 300-page document densely packed with text and intricate diagrams.

In essence, Boyd saw that success in a dogfight (or in business...or in a hot presentation) depends on cycling through your OODA loop faster than the other guy. That way—and this is key—you "get inside" your opponent's OODA loop. Getting inside his OODA loop shakes up his thinking and causes him to make critical errors. The heart of the theory is that it's not necessarily the best decisions that win the game, but the speed with which decisions are made—sort of a variation of not letting the perfect become the enemy of the good. As Sun Tzu noted in *The Art of War*, "I have heard of [successful] military operations that were clumsy but swift, but I have never seen one that was skillful and lasted a long time."[1]

But the essential starting points are those two goose eggs in OODA— Observe and Orient.

---

[1] The Art of War, 1:58 (Dettmer's citation).

OBSERVE:

This is a search for information. The speaker must analyze the audience carefully, getting a clear image of who will be listening. What is it that *they*—not you—are most interested in hearing about in this particular forum? What are they *not* likely to be interested in? What is their emotional temperature? (Are they complacent, anxious, desperate?) Why should they care about your company? Or about what it's doing? Or how it's doing it?

Know your opposition. What are their main marketing messages? How exactly have they been trying to differentiate themselves? What have they been saying in their own executive presentations? Their ads? Their sales material? Their remarks in the trade press? As Sun Tzu tells us, "Unless you know the mountains and forests, the defiles and impasses, and the lay of the marshes and swamps, you cannot maneuver with an armed force."[2]

Another way to get inside your opponent's OODA loop is by seeing to it that at least some of the information you have will be information that your adversary does not have. Management guru H. William Dettmer puts it this way: "What you're looking for—what you can best capitalize on—are data that don't fit with your current orientation, or worldview (and especially the worldview of your opponent). It is these 'mismatches' that offer the potential for learning something that your adversaries don't know, thereby creating a tactical advantage that you can exploit."[3]

[2] The Art of War, 1:116 (Dettmer's citation).
[3] H. William Dettmer, "Operationalizing Sun Tzu: The OODA Loop"

ORIENT:

Here you are synthesizing the information just gained from observations and generating an updated picture of reality. To the extent that you can synthesize a more accurate picture of reality than your opponent can, the quality of your decisions and actions will be that much better.

With only a week to prepare your presentation, the temptation you will face is to skip the OO and go straight to the DA. Fight that. Because then you'd be flying blind. Colonel Boyd would not consider that a good idea in a dogfight.

CHAPTER EIGHT:
SECURE THE OBJECTIVE.

"The most dangerous moment comes with victory."

— NAPOLEON BONAPARTE

CHAPTER EIGHT:
SECURE THE OBJECTIVE.

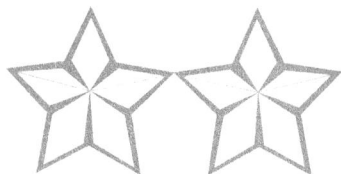

TELL THEM WHAT HAPPENED AND WHAT'S NEXT.

Take this five-second test. It consists of two questions. First: How many presentations have you sat through as a member of an audience? Write the number down in the margin of this book. Second question: How many of those presentations can you remember? Write that number down next to the first number.

> **"**No listener follows you or understands you as perfectly as you would like.**"**

The gap between those numbers is caused by a lot of things. Poor presentations, hazy unfocused presentations, and presentations that were so full of information as to be beyond the reach of anyone watching them.

Almost all those problems can be trumped with a simple but powerful ending to your presentation. In tactical military terms, you need to secure the objective. No battle goes perfectly according to plan. When the battle is over, everyone needs to be told what happened. It is only slightly less so with presentations. No listener follows you or understands you as perfectly as you would like. (Again, the ear is one-tenth the organ of the eye.) Even relatively simple presentations (the quarterly results, for example) can be misunderstood.

Therefore, at the end of your presentation, you need to tell them, in a foreshortened manner, what you just told them. This often means you need to tell them what happens next. What's the next step? How is the future going to change based on what you just told them? These are the vitals the audience needs to take home with them. The "What happens next" point may be something that affects them, directly or indirectly. It doesn't matter. What matters is that you are going to connect the dots—the dots between what you just told them and what comes next BECAUSE of what you just told them.

THREE EXAMPLES OF HOW TO SECURE THE OBJECTIVE:

When you are presenting to customers and other "outside" audiences, your ending can't be a command, as in "Here's what you must do now." But it can be, politically and politely, a question. Here's an example:

A senior executive at a large IT company has just presented his company's next-generation thinking to a large audience of customers and potential customers. In the course of thirty-five minutes, he has presented all the wonderful things his company is now doing, and the kind of great results they are getting from all their innovations. He has "captured" his audience with a compelling presentation. Now he needs to secure his objective. But he can't fall back on the hackneyed, "I think all of you should buy our product and get the same kinds of results we are getting." That would be weak...and forgettable.

Instead, he ends his presentation with a short list of questions— questions that go right to the bottom-line of any major business. He asked three questions in order to "secure the objective:"

1. What are your IT professionals working on? Maintenance or innovation?

2. Can you quantify the business benefits of every expenditure you are making?

3. Do you know if the support you are getting is cost effective?

Then he said "thank you for your time," and "if you remember nothing else I said today, please remember this, thank you for your business." An old-fashioned kind of closing but a good one.

While "thank you for your business" generally gets a closing round of applause, the majority of senior people in the audience are left asking themselves one or more of his "secure the objective" questions.

The next two examples come from the political realm; each offers a clear example of a speaker ending his presentation with a charge to his audience that is clear and compelling and that answers the question: What's next?

This is Jesse Jackson ending his "Keep Hope Alive" speech at the Democratic National Convention in Atlanta, Georgia, in 1988. Jackson was speaking to minorities across the United States. His message was about "not accepting inequality in America." This is how he ended:

> *You must not surrender. You may or may not get there, but just know that you are qualified and you hold on and hold out. We must never surrender. America will get better and better. Keep hope alive. Keep hope alive. Keep hope alive.*

In the spring of 2009, British Prime Minister Gordon Brown spoke to a joint session of the American Congress. His purpose was to implore America and Americans to work with the rest of the world, and with the United Kingdom in particular, to end the world economic crisis and to create new jobs and new wealth for the future of a greener planet. His words were plainly crafted, yet his thoughts and the net impact of his presentation were eloquent. Notice his use of three "Let us" phrases in the ending. His final paragraph is a reprise of the full text of his speech:

> *In the depths of the Depression, when Franklin Roosevelt did battle with fear itself, it was not simply by the power of his words, his personality and his example that he triumphed.*

Yes, all these things mattered. But what mattered more was this enduring truth: that you, the American people, at your core, were, as you remain, every bit as optimistic as your Roosevelts, your Reagans and your Obamas.

This is the faith in the future that has always been the story and promise of America. So at this defining moment in history let us renew our special relationship for our generation and our times. Let us restore prosperity and protect this planet and, with faith in the future, let us together build tomorrow today.

One final piece of advice in the tactical warfare of giving a presentation: Like a skirmish in a war, your next presentation will be only one event in a long line of events needed to achieve victory. Be neither too exhilarated nor too discouraged by the outcome. Remember what worked and what did not work, and prepare for the next skirmish.

Good luck.

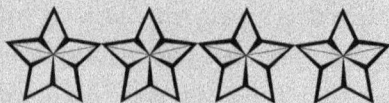

GENERAL DOUGLAS MACARTHUR

Douglas MacArthur holds a unique place in American military history. He ranks as one of the most prepossessing generals the country ever fielded, and one of the very best. He led American troops in action in Mexico (in 1914), in Europe in World War I, across the entire Southwest Pacific in World War II, and across the Korean Peninsula during the Korean War. Famous for his "I shall return" speech in 1941, during the early days of World War II, when the Japanese Imperial armies and navies swept American forces out of the Philippines, MacArthur rallied the forces necessary to mount the long campaign to retake the Southwest Pacific and help bring an end to the War.

He combined intellect with a warrior spirit—graduating top of his class at West Point—and a keen understanding of how public relations and showmanship play important roles in a military that reports to elected civilian leadership. He served as the Army's first information officer, writing and overseeing press releases from headquarters in Washington, D.C., just before World War I. The son of an Army lieutenant general, he grew up with first-hand knowledge of the politics and relationships that supplement a successful military career at the higher ranks.

In World War I, he flouted the strict uniform rules and wore bright turtleneck sweaters and elaborate scarves. He got away with it because everyone knew that he was "something special"—a top West Point graduate and the son of a Lieutenant General. It almost cost him his life once. But instead of shooting first and asking questions later, a soldier from another division came across him on the battlefield and merely took him prisoner, thinking he might be a German officer.

So the general's antics and famous speeches made him a favorite among the general population. Not nearly as well known is that he earned the right to strut his stuff.

At Veracruz, Mexico, in 1914 he went on a long-range reconnaissance mission where, ambushed several times, he had to shoot his way out, making his way back to safety with three or four bullet holes in his uniform. He was nominated for the Medal of Honor for that effort, but did not receive it.

In World War I, where he became the Army's youngest Brigadier General, he repeatedly went on raids and attacks with his soldiers, exposing himself to enemy fire and poisonous gas often enough to earn him seven Silver Stars, the Army's third-highest combat award, and a Distinguished Service Cross, the second highest.

Finally, amidst controversy, he did receive the Medal of Honor for his efforts to initially defend the Philippines against the Japanese invasion. (Interesting aside: when he got the Medal of Honor, he and his father became the only father and son generals to both receive it. His dad,

Arthur MacArthur, won his at the Battle of Missionary Ridge under General Ulysses S. Grant during the American Civil War.)

Even into his sixties and seventies, during World War II and Korea, he exposed himself to enemy fire to see for himself how the troops were doing. He had every right to talk to his soldiers in war language soldiers understand. So in addition to the poetic lines he is famous for (e.g., "Old soldiers never die, they just fade away") he could bring some heavy lead when he needed to.

Once, in the critical days leading to victory in World War I, his own commanding general had told him to take a German strong point in the Argonne Forest called Cote de Chatillon, "or show me a list of 5,000 casualties." MacArthur replied that he would take the German position or his own name would be first on the list.

Flash forward twenty-five years to the South Pacific and World War II. MacArthur's men are bogged down in a swampy slugfest with the Japanese Imperial Army at a dot on the map called Buna, New Guinea. MacArthur summons General Robert Eichelberger to his command center. He tells Eichelberger:

> *Bob, I'm putting you in command at Buna. Relieve Harding ... I want you to remove all officers who won't fight. Relieve regimental and battalion commanders; if necessary, put sergeants in charge of battalions and corporals in charge of companies ... Bob, I want you to take Buna, or not come back alive ... And that goes for your chief of staff, too.*

Eichelberger won the battle of Buna. And came back alive.

IN TODAY'S CONNECTED WORLD,
THE ONLY ONE IN THE ROOM WHO
DOESN'T KNOW HOW WELL HE'S DOING
IS THE ONE MAKING A PRESENTATION.

THAT'S ABOUT TO CHANGE.

INDEX:

ABOUT THE
AUTHORS:

TWO LEADING SPEECHWRITERS - A FORMER U.S. ARMY RANGER
& A U.S. MARINE - REWRITE THE HANDBOOK FOR PRESENTERS

CHUCK BOYER

Chuck Boyer spent 16 years at IBM, where he was manager of corporate publications and editor of the company's THINK Magazine. He has written speeches and white papers for IBM, HP, Compaq, Digital, Symphony Services, MasterCard, and Arthur D. Little Consulting. He has a B.S. in industrial engineering from Penn State University, and was a Company Executive Officer and Ranger in the U.S. Army.

BILL DUNNE

For over 20 years Bill Dunne has been coaching leaders in the private and public sectors and academia in the art and craft of making persuasive presentations. His clients are in industries including information technology, finance, science, engineering, medicine, biotechnology, pharmaceuticals, healthcare, manufacturing, homeland security, and national defense. He holds a bachelor's degree in economics and was a proud U.S. Marine.

FOR MORE INFORMATION:

CREATE SPACE (E-STORE):

http://www.createspace.com/presentationaswar

AMAZON:

http://www.amazon.com
Search "Presentation as War"

WEBSITE:

http://www.presentationaswar.com

FACEBOOK:

http://www.facebook.com/pages/presentation-as-war

TWITTER:

@ChuckBoyer

APPEARANCES

Phone: 1+ 203.853.6665
Email: bdunne@optonline.net or cboyer@somtel.com

ABOUT SPOTLIGHT CREATIVE

Spotlight Creative's expertise lies in helping our clients develop
and present their brand message, and connecting the employee,
partner and customer to the return on their investment. We do this
by creating engaging communication connections, which drives
the emotional bond that motivates brand advocacy, and ultimately,
investment decisions.

www.ingramcontent.com/pod-product-compliance
Lightning Source LLC
Chambersburg PA
CBHW071453200326
41519CB00019B/5723